Flights

of a

Featherbrain

G.T. Warner

ISBN: 978-1-962402-48-4

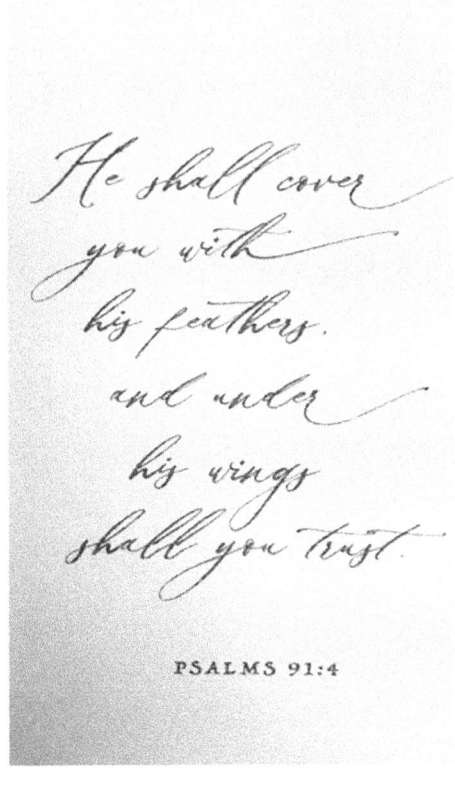

He shall cover
you with
his feathers.
and under
his wings
shall you trust.

PSALMS 91:4

⁷Because you are my help, I sing in the shadow of your wings.
⁸I cling to you; your right hand upholds me."

— Psalm 63:7-8.

Dedication

This book is dedicated to my husband, Steve, the love of my life and soulmate since I was a shy 16-year-old. We have grown up and old together. I am so very blessed and grateful for you and our journey through life side by side.

I also dedicate it to my mother and father, whose lives were a struggle through pain and addiction. There would be no story to tell without them. I think of them often with love. May they rest in peace knowing that I have come to understand and forgive as an adult. I am stable and well. The chain of addiction in our family has been broken.

Thank you Julia Gorecki Hite, (Grannie) 1898 - 1992 for being an inspiration and example in perseverance and faith in God.

Acknowledgment

My heartfelt thanks to my dear husband, Steve who read and listened to these stories many times. You have always been there for me.

Many thanks to my brother, Mark, for the hours of reminiscing our good times and bad times. You helped me add thoughts I had forgotten and photos that I had never seen, to this, our story.

Thank you, Connie Warner Kirkman, my (more like a sister) sister-in-law for your encouragement and making me believe I could and should tell my story each time I felt like giving up.

Thanks to my dear friends, my Beta Readers, who read chapters and gave me feedback: Florence York Ellis, Carol McCue Banker, Cheryl Thomas Radziej, Gail Clifton, Susan Key and Amy Caldwell.

A tremendous Thank You to Karel Fontaine a fellow writer and member of Allison Wearing's *Alumni Café, Memoir Writing, INK.* for your expertise, editing skills and review. Your assistance was invaluable to me.

Contents

CHAPTER ONE

The Featherbrain

"Your daughter is a Featherbrain", my first-grade teacher, declared to my mother. "She spends too much time gazing out of the window during class."

The treasure I found that no one could take away from me was the gift of dissociating when bored or anxious due to mundane or chaotic happenings that I had no other way to escape. My six-year-old attention span often flew out the window like a fluttering bird while I sat on the hard little wooden chairs listening to my classmates repeat, "Look, Jane, look" and "Go Spot, Go." in our first-grade, *Dick and Jane Readers*. I was able to retreat this way at school or go deep within at home when the raging rants of my alcoholic father and depressed, border line personality Mother became unbearable.

I am grateful that I learned to slip into the heart of my soul in silence where I often found creative thoughts and a peace that I realized much later was from God.

Now, seventy years later, I still take featherbrained flights, remembering with a chuckle the incidences that turned into laughter instead of tears, the fear and anxiety that made me strong. I am grateful for the moments that God worked in my life. The family curse of alcoholism and drugs passed down from our great-grandfathers, grandfathers to parent and on to a sibling has been broken. My sisters, brother, and I became stronger and more compassionate with others due to our struggles, the good, the bad, the frightening. I have been blessed with the priceless gift of finding peace and beauty in small things. Love is always near and overflowing.

The aroma of strong black coffee takes me to my childhood kitchen on a cold winter morning. Bird song triggers a featherbrained flight back to my dining room window seat eating toast before going to elementary school. The smell of smoke from a crackling, red-hot bonfire on a winter day transports me to the icy feeling of frigid air and tingly ice crystals being sucked in through my nose and down into my lungs when Dad and I put on ice skates and swirled around the frozen pond at the city park. The way sunlight casts a dreamy shadow at dusk also awakens my memory to incidents in years and places long ago. My heart and soul are then filled to overflowing with profound gratitude and thanks to God for the end of this story.

Mother glared at me with furrowed brows in the hall outside my first-grade classroom when my teacher, a Holy Humility of Mary Nun, called me a featherbrain. I kept my eyes fixated at the large black rosary beads with silver crucifix at my teachers waist not wanting to look at her for fear of crying. As I held back tears, I ran my tongue around my teeth trying to ignore the lump in my throat. I was determined not to cry. When I got home from school that day, Mom made sure I knew of her displeasure as she declared, "The heat of humiliation rose up my neck in a hot, red blush when she called you a featherbrain! You really embarrassed me! It didn't help the situation that you stood there running your tongue around the inside of your mouth and rolling your eyes like marbles in a cup as though you were not mentally capable!" Hearing my mother's pain due to my actions embarrassed me and put me into a state of not wanting to face that teacher or the classroom ever again.

This incident was a forgotten memory of the past until I started journaling things I remembered from my childhood and realized how often my featherbrained self has been touched, influenced, or rescued by creatures with feathers. If I were a person who believed in Indian Totems, my Spirit Animal would be an Owl, according to a questionnaire I answered online. There have been many birds or perhaps angels appearing as birds in my life. Encounters with feathered friends and the beauty of their flight and mine have guided me to ponder, search for truth and seek wisdom.

CHAPTER TWO

Gooney Bird

T o begin with, Dad called me *"Gooney Bird"* when I was small and this is how it came to be:

To say my father swore like a sailor was correct on two counts. He did, and he had been. He was an 18-year-old High School Senior when he dropped out on his March birthday and signed up to join the war effort in 1942. He was proud of his tour of duty as a Pharmacist Mate aboard The USS *St. George* in WWll. He had no clue how his desire to serve his country would affect his entire life and the lives of his future family.

I never asked why he called me *Gooney Bird* when I was little. It wasn't until I researched his tour in the Pacific more than 50 years later that I read about the *Gooney Bird*; until then, I didn't know it was a real bird! I thought it was just a silly name he made up for me. The *Gooney Bird* is not gooney at all. It is a Black-Footed Albatross. They fly high for long periods of time, riding strong air currents. You might say they depend on God's power to soar.

The *Gooney Bird* is one of the most graceful sea birds when flying. I thought he called me *Gooney Bird* because he thought I was gooney. I didn't like it! When I was 10, and he'd call me "*Gooney Bird*," I would say, "NO! You are a *Gooney Bird*," and we would laugh. I found a clip of this bird trying to take off and land during my research. It resembles how a toddler tries to take off and often lands with their bottom hitting the floor with a thud. It made me think that perhaps he was not making fun of my awkwardness as a very young child. I choose to believe it was more likely an endearing term as he watched my determination to fly from one side of the room to the other and land with a thud!

I am told I was not a child who sat still. I was constantly moving. I flitted around dancing, jumping, twirling like a whirling dervish. When I saw the clip of this bird soaring gracefully and landing with a THUD, I realized that I may have misunderstood why he called me *Gooney Bird* when I was young. I misunderstood him. The whole family misunderstood him in so many ways. We had no way of knowing what he lived with daily as a result of the trauma of WWII.

Dad and the Gooney Bird – 1949.

As a child, I had no idea of the connection between his alcoholism and his tour of duty. My mother didn't know either. Dad had broken her heart so many times by embarrassing and terrifying her that she hated him. She thought he was just a crazy drunk, and she told us many times that he was a *psycho alcoholic* and everyone in town looked down on him. "Your last name is a curse because everyone in town knows what an asshole your father is!" There were no other families with our last name in town.

Grannie said, "Hold your head up high and don't pay any attention to what anyone says or the way they look at you. You are just as good as anyone else." What she meant as encouragement made us paranoid that everyone looked down on us." Because no one else in town had our last name, we assumed everyone knew who our father was, and we were embarrassed and ashamed. I learned otherwise as an adult, but if a child believes a parent is no good, it destroys their self-esteem.

Dad studied hard, took his test, and earned his CDT – (Certified Dental Technician) certificate. The certificate came in the mail one day. Mom opened the envelope and laughingly told us, "CDT, Cities Dumbest Turd for sure!" I was proud of him for attaining the goal he had worked so hard for and upset that my mother made fun of him. As an adult, I realize Mom's Borderline Personality caused her to lash out with unkind accusations and ravings. The things she said and the way she tried to manipulate us was as bad and sometimes worse than the alcoholism. We were all unaware of her illness and believed her every word.

CHAPTER THREE

Find Your Happy Place

This morning the aroma of my cup of coffee transported me to the memory of my mother sitting again at the yellow Formica Table with her cup in one hand and a cigarette in the other, taking pills to ease her pain. She often stared into her cup as though she was searching for answers like the colorfully dressed, fortune telling gypsy lady I saw at the Lake County Fair. It seemed her point of focus was on trying to make herself feel better amid the alcoholic hell that we were all experiencing. One of her favorite sayings while taking another drag on her *Tareyton* was in exact contrast to her distraught mood, "Everyone needs to find their Happy Place." Her happy place may have been sitting at that table with a cup of coffee and a cigarette because she spent a lot of time there.

Mom's pain was both physical and emotional. The torment of Dad's alcoholism caused her to suffer unrelenting migraines. The bitterness in her heart towards him was stronger than any acrid bite of blackest coffee; it ate at her heart and soul. She saw no way out of the deep darkness that smothered her. Divorce was out of the question because the church forbade it. Catholic Doctrine before the Second  Vatican Council stated that "The church condemns divorce as immoral, a grave offense against the natural law which injures the covenant of salvation, and is considered a plague on society." We were enveloped in her sadness every time we looked at the empty blank look of her steely gray-blue eyes.

The high-ceilinged, bead-boarded, yellow-and-white kitchen needed a good coat of paint to cover the years of all that smoke swirling madly and mixing with the steamy aroma of greasy burgers, sloppy joes, cabbage rolls and fried fish on Friday. The black and green marbled linoleum floor slanted slightly towards the back of the house due to the settling of our 100- year -old home.

We four would take our only pair of roller skates that had been Mom's as a teenager and took turns giving each other a push to roll towards the back wall of the kitchen. It was fun to see who could remain standing as we hit the wall. Now I can say, we all *hit the wall* as adults, and we are all still standing! The floor gave out a little when we kids jumped up and down. It became a game to see who could jiggle the joists the most. We found our fun in oddly creative ways. The foundation of our home, built in 1846, had settled and shifted somewhat through the years. The foundation was crumbling and so was our family in 1956.

Grannie Julia and Grandpa George lived in a two-room cottage on the property that dad had remodeled. It was situated across the driveway from our home. George and Julia moved to town when Grannie made the down payment to purchase the place instead of Mom, Dad and us four kids continuing to rent and live in the upstairs apartment.

The New York Central train depot was on the other side of the field behind our house. It was easy for Grannie to walk across the field every weekday morning and cross Railroad Street to the train station. The train would take her to downtown Cleveland where she worked at a drug store. In the evening she would ride the train back to Painesville.

Conveniently for my dad and Grandpa George it was the same short walk across that field to the *The Depot Café*. It was a bar that they often frequented. It is still located on Railroad Street right across from the old train depot.

Grandpa George was a Creative Alcoholic Curmudgeon, proof of which is in Chapter Ten. He was highly intelligent but lacking in common courtesy and common sense. He drank heavily and although he tried to stop drinking several times, he never succeeded.

The last time he tried in 1945 he had the DTs so badly that he jumped out of a third story window at a Veterans Hospital in Cleveland, Ohio, and broke his leg. Gangrene set in and it had to be amputated. He loved to shock and disturb our friends by taking a drag on his Camel Cigarette, lifting the leg of his pants and flicking the ashes in the hole in his wooden leg. We hoped and prayed he would never set himself on fire!

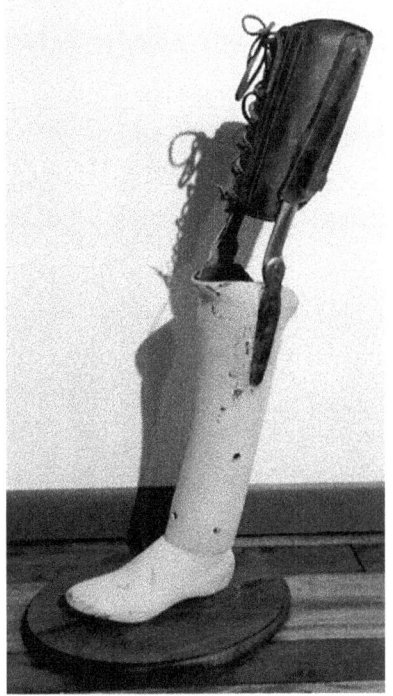

CHAPTER FOUR

Looking for Happy

Mom's advice to "Find our Happy Place" was taken to heart by all of us. We all had our temporary Happy Places.

My father's Happy Place was working in his vegetable garden in the back yard. I can still see his big, darkly tanned hands, grimy from digging in the dirt, wrapped around a brown glass bottle of Pabst Blue Ribbon Beer.

He'd take several gulps and let out a sigh as he placed the bottle firmly in the dirt up against a tomato stake or a bean pole to balance it as he continued to pull weeds while on his knees. I knew he had to be thirsty out in the sun by the sweat running into his dark bushy eyebrows. I wished he was drinking lemonade instead of that beer. After he was finished gardening, he would take the empty bottle and throw it down the well in the very back of our yard. The well had dried up years before Grannie, Mom and Dad had bought the house in 1956. It was an excellent place to hide those bottles. Mom hardly ever went outside due to her very fair skin and her hatred for bugs so she would never see the collection of amber glass glistening in the sun. Despite the heat and the sweat, he was smiling.

His other Happy Place was sitting in a nearby bar. Sometimes my brother or I sat with him as we savored a salty pretzel and a sweet, icy cold Coke sipped through a straw. "Were you thirsty from that pretzel" he would ask with a grin? "Glad, we stopped for a drink, aren't you?"

We crunched and sipped while listening to the jukebox of 50s tunes in the dark, smoky lounge. The cherry red and shiny silver jukebox in the darkest corner played 45s like "Que Sera Sera" (Whatever will be will be) sung by Doris Day or *Jailhouse Rock* by Elvis Presley. These two songs in particular, made me ponder. I pondered a lot as a child. "Que Sera Sera, whatever will be. The future's not ours to see, Que Sera Sera." Were we all destined to accept whatever happened to us as Doris Day sang, or could prayer change the course of the events of our lives like the nuns and priest told us. Were our lives predestined with no hope of making things better? Jail House Rock made me smile, but I didn't tell Daddy why. I imagined Daddy dancing with joy the day Grannie and I bailed him out of jail on a cold icy January Morning.

He was a good dancer and so was Mom. I remember them dancing and laughing just once. My sister, Lill, won a stereo record player in 1958 at the St. Mary's Lawn Fete. Mom had purchased four of the raffle tickets I brought home from school and had put each of our names on one of them. I was there in the schoolyard when they called Lill's name and I ran home to get Dad. It was too big and heavy for me to carry.

As soon as he brought it into the house he started hunting in the closets. He said he was looking for a crate that had their old 78s. Turns out 78s were big black discs that you put on a turntable or record player and the room was filled with music. I was used to our little red or black 45s that we kids played. I had never seen these big black records before. That evening was the first and only time I felt love in the room with Mom and Dad. He had not been drinking for a while, so even Mom was in a good mood! He swirled Mom around like an egg beater, and their feet hardly touched the floor! Dad said the name of the tune was *Little Brown Jug*. Mom said, out of breath and laughing, "It's called the *Jitterbug*. We danced like this the first time we met in a bar in downtown Cleveland." She said they danced most of that night and many nights after that. They got married just three months later on September 23, 1947. I entered the world on June 24, 1948. This is my only memory of them looking at each other, and smiling.

Dancing at Uncle Paul and Aunt Elaine's Wedding in 1953.

I was always uncomfortable sitting in a bar. My favorites were *Tony's Subway Inn* by the railroad tracks on State Street or the *Depot Café* on Railroad Street. I knew I would probably lie to Mom when we got home when she asked me if Dad had gone to a bar. She habitually asked me whenever I went anywhere with him if he had stopped at a bar. I always felt I was partly to blame because I enjoyed the pretzel and coke so very much. I was thirsty too, and I didn't want them to fight again. If I lied, I would have to tell the priest that I lied to my mother when I went to confession on Saturday afternoon. You never knew which priest was behind that tiny cloth-covered screen in the dark confessional. Some of the priests were kinder than others but waiting in line always sent my heart into hard and fast palpitations that would make me lightheaded with anxiety. Father Sidley didn't understand when I told him once that I hated my father sometimes, but I couldn't help it. He asked me why and I didn't know how to explain. I just said my father scared me. If I told him I lied to my mother he wouldn't understand why I did that either. In my mind, it was the lesser of two evils. I didn't want to tell the truth because the truth would make things worse again. I knew better than to get anything started between my parents. It was the lesser of two evils to lie and face the wrath of God and Fr. Sidley, who I knew, would just tell me to say Five Our Fathers and Five Hail Mary's rather than face the fury of my fighting parents; the screaming, smashing things against walls and the fear of seeing them tear into each other was too much for me.

Was it possible that prayer could change the course of the events of our lives? I was determined things would get better. Answered prayer was proven to me many years later as I sat again at *Tony's Subway Inn* near that same noisy railroad track, eating spaghetti and meatballs while listening to *Never My Love* by The Association in 1968 with my future husband.

"Never My Love" became our song that night. The words are still valid for us 55 years later.

> *"You ask me if there'll come a time*
> *When I'll grow tired of you*
> *Never, my love*
> *Never, my love*
> *You wonder if this heart of mine*
> *will lose its desire for you*
> *Never, my love."*

CHAPTER FIVE

Fatso and Peaches

My sister Lill's happy place was behind a big red, wingback chair in the corner of the living room with her fairy tale books or sitting on our dining room window seat watching the birds in our yard. Her favorite book was by *Hans Christian Anderson*. She loved the brightly colored illustrations of *Twelve Dancing Princesses*, who danced at an exquisite palace all night long in beautiful gowns. Another of her favorites was the story of *The Ugly Duckling*, who turned into an elegantly feathered swan. Her four-year-old self was skinny and freckled with red untamed hair.

As an adult she became the most classy and beautiful of us three sisters. Because she was only four and didn't read, I read these stories to her many times until it got to the point where she remembered the words and pretended she was reading them by herself. The colorful illustrations cued her to the sequence of the story. I liked the *Princesses and Swan* stories, but I did not like *The Poor Little Match Girl* or *Thumbelina*. Those stories in particular made me and Lill very sad. Was there a connection between the ending of "Thumbelina" and Lill's fascination with watching the birds at our dining room window seat?

> *"Farewell, farewell," said the swallow, with a heavy heart,*
> *as he left the warm countries to fly back into Denmark.*
> *There he had a nest over the window of a house where the*

*writer of fairy tales lived. The swallow sang "Tweet, tweet,"
and from his song came this whole story."*
—Hans Christian Anderson

Lill sat on the drafty window seat snuggly wrapped in a blanket of baby blue peering out through the frosty window. Air flowing from the nearby furnace vent gently stirred her soft red curls with currents of warmth. She was entranced by branches full of chattering winter wrens. Two little wrens made a nest under the eve of our picture window. The little *sputzies*, as Grannie called them, were waiting for the Cardinals and Blue Jays to finish feeding on crumbs and crusts Mom had thrown onto the snow-covered driveway. The big, noisy, aggressive birds often frightened the tiny birds, forcing them to fly off and hide in the safety of the thick branches of a nearby pine. When the big birds had flown out of sight, the little ones returned from their safe hiding places to feed their hunger.

Mom named these feathered breakfast visitors, Fatso and Peaches just for the fun of it. Fatso because he was bigger and rounder than his feathered mate, and Peaches because she had a slightly peachy, beige tinge to her tan and brown feathers. We watched them in the morning while eating our oatmeal, and toast with

Lil, 5, standing with Gail, 8.

the peach jam that Grannie and I made from peaches we gathered in the back yard the summer before.

Fatso and Peaches were fluffing their feathers bravely and clenching their icy perches tightly as great gusts of frigid wind blew the branches they clung to. The little wrens maintained their controlled grip as the wind blew violently. The shaking and blowing caused huge dollops of sparkling white balanced on branches from the previous night's snowstorm to fall occasionally in great clumps on the ground. The blobs of ice-covered snow dropping to the ground scared the big birds away; only then would the little ones descend to the driveway to eat. When the big birds flew back, the sputzies would retreat again to the safety of their icy perches. I understood their fearful, quick retreats back to safety because we, too, had learned to run and hide when the loud shouting and angry smashing of objects on walls frightened us.

As an adult I sense the commonality we had with our little bird friends. Our unconscious desire was to maintain some control and not get blown away by the blasts of anger and drunkenness that were a part of our childhood. Like our birds, we tried to stay out of the way and hold on tightly to the hope that things would change.

I tried to hear what my sister said while she gazed out the window. She was whispering in quiet conversational tones when I overheard. "Fly away, Hurry, be safe, Fly away!!"

She was much quieter and more easily frightened than I was, so I wasn't surprised by her words. She was a pale, thin, ginger-haired beauty. Her skin had a fair translucence that allowed tiny blue veins to be visible through her skin at her temples and wrists. Her little fingernails reminded me of my first rosary's tiny pink oval beads. "Delicate" is what Grannie called her. "You be good to your sister now…She is so thin and delicate she probably won't live long." Then I would be told the story, once again, of how Grannie had lost three of her seven sisters in the flu epidemic of 1918 and how she still felt guilt over things she had said and done, even after going to confession.

For years, I was concerned and convinced that if I wasn't "good to my sister," not upset her, and let her have her way, she might die. Since I was older by three and a half years, I "should know better" than to cause her to be upset. I needed to be responsible for my behavior. I was told I needed to be an excellent example to my younger siblings. Yes, "I should know better" was a phrase I repeatedly heard as a child. No wonder, as an adult, I still berated myself for not "knowing better" about many things and doing better with everything!

I didn't want to be blamed for being the one who started something that I would regret later when Dad or Mom got angry. Decades later I still admonished myself with unrelenting "should have known betters!" I tried to "Know Better." I learned to give in quickly to keep peace in the family and often took responsibility and blame for things that really weren't my fault. It was no wonder that, as an adult, I still berated myself for not "knowing better" about many things! If only I had met Sister Mary Clare in my childhood instead of at the age of 50 at a silent ten-day Contemplative Prayer Retreat. She smilingly told me, "When something is said or done it is over and in the past, God does not want us to 'should' on ourselves."

I asked Lill, "Who are you talking to? Are you making up a story like *The Snow Queen* that I read to you last night? She turned around and said, "The birds, I'm talking to the birds … and they are talking with me! I am not making up stories."

"Birds don't talk," I replied.

She glared at me, "They do too! They tell me secrets and things." "Really… like… what kind of things? You must be imagining. We've been reading those fairy tales you like so much lately. It's good to have an imagination!

"I'm NOT making this up," she replied.

Being older and more realistic, I didn't delve into her fantasy world of fairies, elves, and talking birds. I knew the difference between silly hopes, dreams, bird stories, and reality; I just knew better and said so. I am still a person who does not sugar coat reality.

"No one can hear birds talk because birds don't talk! They make bird noises, Twitter, and Chirp, not words people can understand." Seeing her eyebrows drawn together and her pouty lip protruding, I softened my tone, knowing better than to make her angry. Then I thought that what she might be hearing could be an angel. Grannie says angels sometimes talk to us and give us ideas and messages in our minds, even though we cannot see them. Hearing angels only happens when we are still and listen for a small, quiet voice inside our hearts. Angels might be real. Believing there were angels around to help when needed was a comforting thought.

Sister Mary Bernice said we all have a guardian angel of our own to watch over us and protect us. I hoped it was true. It gave me a good, safe feeling to know there might be invisible help when needed.

"Look, Angels like this!" Using my fingernail as though it were a stylus, I gently scraped an outline of an angel in the frost that had accumulated inside the glass window pane. The stinging ice stuck between the creatively inspired finger and its sturdy fingernail. It felt like a frozen needle jamming into my fingertip. Having no storm windows to keep out the moisture made a wintery etch-a-sketch out of the panes on this side of the house.

Enjoying the artistic muse, I ignored the cold sting, and ice angels multiplied one after another. As the sun peeked from behind a massive snow cloud, a ray of light fell through the window, giving the angels a radiant look that made me think, *Yes, angels might be real!* I wondered if it really could be angels instead of birds talking to her.

My brother told me his Happy Place was in the kitchen close to Mom at the table where she often sat. There was a low three-foot by three-foot cupboard where Mom kept our boots and old shoes by the back door. He was only three, so he could easily crawl into that low closet with his flashlight and hide. Whenever we couldn't find him, he would be in his happy place.

He liked it because he could see Mom at the kitchen table through a crack in that cupboard door and he felt safe. Just being close enough to see her made him feel secure. He hated being far from Mom even to the point of not wanting to go to school when he was old enough to go to kindergarten.

It was my job to take him the three blocks and then turn to go to my own class to the school in the next block after he was safe inside his classroom. He often broke loose from my grip and ran away from me towards home, then the chase would ensue. He always ran faster than I could! I wished every day that Mom would take him so I wouldn't have to worry about being late for school. It was the year I was in fourth grade and I had Sister Mary Anne! She had no grace for those who were late to class!

My preferred happy place was outside climbing our Peach Tree or the big old Cherry Tree behind the barn in the summer. I would sit high up in the boughs where no one could see me. I loved the bitter-sweet aroma of pink blossoms in the spring and fruit-laden branches in the summer. Hiding in the branches and listening to bird song filled me with hope as I looked out and beyond our present home life. There was more out there in the world and someday I would grow up and away.

In the winter, I would make snow angels or slide on the ice in our driveway pretending to be an Olympic Skater and remembering the fun I had when Dad took me down to the flats to ice skate.

We rented skates at the city Recreation Center. A big bonfire burned in the flats next to the pond where you could warm up and drink hot chocolate or coffee. The smell of wood burning in the chill winter air brings back this warm memory of my dad from more than 60 years ago.

I was amazed at how couples were whizzing past us holding hands and gliding around and around as they circled the iced-over pond. At first, my ankles were wobbly like spaghetti noodles so Dad tightened up the laces of my skates until my ankles couldn't wobble anymore. He held my hand and wrapped his arm around me to keep me from falling. He had not been drinking, so I wasn't afraid of him those two nights as we slowly glided around the frozen pond. I got pretty good at going forward, but as hard as he tried to teach me to skate backwards, I could never do it. He said, "It's OK if you never learn to go backwards, because going forward is more important than looking back and going backwards."

Jade was happy whenever I picked her up, played peek a boo and other little games. I carried her around a lot, pretending she was my baby. I felt I was her "little mother" and looked after her when Mom was flat out on her bed with a migraine or staring out into space with that faraway look in her eyes. Some mornings I would go to her crib as she sat quietly playing with a stuffed toy. I would greet her with "Good morning, J Bird! Whose baby are you? Her reply was, "Gao's baby." As an adult Jade doesn't remember anything about the days when our dad still lived with us. She has blocked it all out permanently.

St. Mary's church, a few houses down the block was a place I went often as one of my happy places. It was easy to run down the street and slip into the cool dark sanctuary to kneel in silence. The sight and smell of flickering votive candles and the residue of smoldering incense calmed my heart and soul as though God wrapped a blanket of love and peace on my shoulders.

Some children may have had fantasies of *Santa Claus*, the *Tooth Fairy*, or dreams of Disneyland in the 1950s. My favorite flight of imagination was to grow up and away to a place of my own. It would be a beautiful home with a loving husband who did not drink. My husband would be gentle and kind. My children would not be afraid because there would be no fights and fits of rage. My children would feel safe and loved. The house would be clean and cheerful with lots of food in the cupboards, sunshine through clean windows, music, and curtains that matched the bedspreads like a friend of mine had in her room. It would be a place filled with love and peace. It would be my Forever Happy Place!

CHAPTER SIX

Long Dark Hair

My long dark hair reached way past my shoulders. Mom always pulled my thick mop into a single ponytail high on my head in the heat of summer. Because of Mom's migraines I often walked to the corner store to purchase things we needed from the time I was seven years old.

Sometimes I walked with a sashay, shifting my shoulders and hips so the banded hair would swing from left to right, gracing each shoulder with a swish. Counting how many times I could keep the rhythm going was fun. *Left, right, left-right.* It was a game for me like, *Step on a crack, and you'll break your mother's back.* I often avoided each crack on the sidewalk as I walked to and from school, Mass or the little Italian *Mom and Pop* store at the corner of Erie and Elm.

The owners of DiCarlo's corner store were first generation Italians. I had some second-generation Italian friends and I loved to play with them, but Mr. and Mrs. DiCarlo were scary to me! I couldn't understand the loud lyrical language that they shot back and forth between them like a ping-pong ball on fire!

I had learned to stay away from people screaming and flailing arms around. It frightened me. Going into the store was worth it. I knew I would walk out with a penny candy or a five-cent popsicle to eat on the way home. Blueberry Blue was my favorite. It was frosty, cold and tasty and the same color as my Uncle Paul's Baby Blue Edsel.

I wasn't walking my unique way that hot summer day in '58. I hurried to get there and back home as quickly as possible because Mom had another migraine. I was running to the corner store to get a half-pound of bologna sliced thin and a loaf of Wonder Bread to make sandwiches for my sisters and brother.

The best thing about Dad's vegetable garden in the backyard was the big red, juicy beefsteak tomatoes. Bologna, tomato, and mayonnaise sandwiches were a tasty summertime staple. As soon as I got home, I would make sandwiches and Red Kool-Aid for the four of us.

Clutching my mom's note asking the shop owners to give me a pack of *Tareytons*, bologna and bread, I opened the old creaky screened door into the bleached and worn wooden-floored grocery. The store had a distinct smell of sawdust and meat. Mom was so sick that she couldn't pull my hair into the usual ponytail! I must have been a hot, sweaty mess with my hair all wild and messy because Mrs. DiCarlo looked at me and said — "Why no ponytail? Too hot to have all that hanging around your neck today! Come Here!" she demanded.

She was a big woman with a big nose and black hair braided and twisted into a bun around the top and back of her head. I wondered how long her hair must be to have it braided and turned around that way. She was almost as old as my Grannie! Her hair must have been very long. The silver-white streaks on both sides of her head reminded me of the racing stripes on cars towed past our old house on RT 20. It was the favored route to get to the nearby races at the Painesville Speedway on Fairport Nursery Road. It was fun to watch the multi-colored cars go by as we sat on our front porch.

I explained about my mom being sick and gave her the note. She looked down her large nose at me and said, "First, let me find a gum band and a brush." I didn't know what a gum band was, but I didn't dare question her. She came to my side of the counter and very gently brushed my hair. Mrs. DiCarlo didn't smile much and sometimes yelled at kids to quit horsing around in the store having her brush my hair made me very uncomfortable.

"I'm sorry your momma sick. Getting your hair up will make your day a little better." I couldn't see what she was doing; there was no mirror to check it out. It did feel better when she finished with me. My neck no longer felt sweaty, with my hair fixed how she styled it. I thanked her, took the cigarettes, bologna, and bread she had placed in a brown paper bag, and left the store.

I looked at my reflection in the storefront window when I got outside. I knew she had parted it in the middle, but I wasn't ready for what I saw looking back at me! I resembled the character on Howdy Doody, *Princess Summer, Fall, Winter, Spring!* I now had two long dark braids fastened with rubber bands on either side of my head. I was not too fond of its look, but it felt better.

After that day, when I went to the corner store for a pack of *Tarey-ton's*, a penny candy or a cool popsicle, I wasn't afraid of Mrs. DiCarlo.

Even though she was loud and had an unattractively big nose, I realized she was a lovely, kind-hearted lady. That day, I learned never to judge people by their looks or what others say about them.

As an adult, remembering those hot summer afternoons, I smile at the difference between my and my grandchildren's childhoods. They gave cigarettes to a seven-year-old child who had walked alone in the afternoon on one of Ohio's busiest east/west routes. Route 20 runs from Boston, Massachusetts, through Euclid Avenue in Cleveland, Ohio, to Astoria, Oregon. I also smile at the slogan of my mother's favorite cigarette brand. "Us *Tareyton* smokers would rather fight than switch!" Yes! Mom would rather fight; she had a lot of fight in her tiny 5' 2" self if you pushed her too far. It always amazed me that she would have the nerve to stand up to my 6' 2" father.

I hurried home to make sandwiches for the kids. The house is quiet when I walk in the front door except for Lassie barking and Timmy's calls for help on the TV. Mom is still out flat and pale. The cold cloth I placed on her forehead before I left is now damp and warm. She mumbles, "Keep the kids quiet for me, OK?"

I think, *I'll try and do my best. I won't go to the library or Margaret and Cheryl's house today. Mom needs me.* Mom's headache days always made me feel very sad and empty.

It's time to make bologna sandwiches and Kool-Aid for all of us. The kids and I may feel better with something in our stomachs.

The fighting starts in the kitchen. Mark was teasing Lill and threatening to punch her if she doesn't give up her seat so he can sit closer to the TV. He chases her into the kitchen and tries to hit her while Lill screams. "Stop it! Leave me alone." He chases her around the yellow laminate kitchen table, and I grab him by the arm, trying to keep him from catching her. As I pivot, holding onto his arm, he breaks loose, and the momentum of our turning bodies hurls him across the kitchen like a bowling ball. He rolls under the heavy white cast iron farm sink. His head hits a pipe, and he starts to wail, "You trying to kill me?" Lill runs and hides, and my mother moans. I cry as I make four sandwiches and a quart of sweet, sugary Cherry Kool-Aid to soothe us. I have failed Mom again. I didn't keep the kids quiet.

After feeding the kids, I retreat again to the highest boughs of the massive old cherry tree out back by the field where hidden and alone, I listen to the peace of bird song. Looking out to the horizon gives me a hopeful perspective. There was more beyond the confines of my neighborhood and family home, and someday I'd be able to venture out and away.

Borrow wings of heart and soul
soar high above your strife
try a new perspective on the
problems in your life.
Soar high into the stratosphere
to quiet, peace, and calm
amidst warm rays and billowy clouds
look down and see earth's ground.

Difficulties in your life
the whole of your life's drama
with a new perspective, shows them
no bigger than a comma.

Many of the problems
we encounter on the way
are not worth surrendering
the joy of one whole day.

Borrow wings of heart and soul
Soar high above the sod
You'll find yourself experiencing
the Peace that is of God.

— GTW 2012

CHAPTER SEVEN

Heaven or Hell

Mentioning Sister Mary Anne at a class reunion brings everyone to a shudder and then laughter remembering this poor old nun who terrorized us but taught us respect in the process.

Third Grade students prayed they would not be assigned to her class the following year. The first day of school we stood in the schoolyard, some alone, some with parents, waiting to hear our name called. We were to line up behind the nun who called our name. There were tears and downcast looks if Sister Mary Anne called you to her flock. We were to follow her into the church for our opening Mass and Prayers to start the new school year and if you were called to her class the dread and fear of a year with her made you pray harder than you ever had before.

Older siblings and friends told us we better behave. She had the right arm of a Cleveland Indians Pitcher and did not hesitate to aim and throw a wooden and felt chalkboard eraser at a child who was misbehaviing in class. She was known to give the girls a hard, fast slap across the face and when it happened to me, I had no idea what I had done to deserve it! If a boy was taken to the cloakroom to be reprimanded, we heard shouts and the sound of scuffling and bouncing off of walls.

One young man in particular was removed from our school by his parents after a bout with Sister Mary Anne in the cloakroom that turned into a fist fight. Yes, he punched her in self-defense! He grew up to be a respected Army Sergeant 1ˢᵗ Class. He was a supervisor at Unit Training and Equipment, Ravenna, Ohio when he retired. He raised a good solid family and volunteered for several good causes.

After Leroy left St. Mary's and was placed in the nearby public school in the next block, Sister Mary Anne told us we needed to pray for the salvation of the souls of the children who attended public school one street over from St. Mary's. They were not Catholic and had no chance of going to heaven. We should thank God that we were born into the right Catholic Families. I wondered how God could play favorites when HE was the Creator of us all. It didn't seem right that they had no chance for heaven because they weren't born into the right family. I guessed my own dad hadn't been born into the right family because he was not Catholic. If this were true, he was not going to heaven either! This horrified me until I came upon the verse that God doesn't play favorites. Romans 2:11. This confirmed the intuitive thought in my mind on the walk home from school that day when snow was falling softly, placing a clean layer of sparkling dust on the frozen crunchy crust that had been there for days.

Silently I prayed. *Please God I know I'm just a kid and don't understand much of anything but surely you won't send my Dad to hell.* As I walked on, I noticed a small, flat, sheet of ice balanced on top of one of the snow mounds that looked like a misshapen heart. My mittened hand picked it up and began to gently  smooth the edges into a more perfect shaped heart as the words formed in my mind. *If God so loved the world…Surely God's heart could not be as icy cold as this heart of ice that I held in my hand.* How could God shut some of his children out when he wanted us to love each other as we loved ourselves and most importantly HIM? We are all Children of God and we are to love our neighbors as ourselves. I would not say it out loud but I decided Sister Mary Anne must be wrong.

This, of course, was in contrast to what I was being told by Sister Mary Anne. If I asked Father Sidley how God would only allow Catholics in heaven, I would hear the admonition I had heard before when asking questions about things I was being taught but didn't understand. "Who do you think you are, young lady? You dare to question the knowledge of learned men who have given us their wisdom for centuries! "Insolence! Say five Our Fathers and five Hail Mary's." End of conversation.

> "There will be trouble and distress for every human being who does evil; first for the Jew, then for the Gentile; but glory, honor and peace for everyone who does good; first for the Jew, and then for the Gentile, *For God does not show favoritism.*"
>
> —Romans 2:9-11

A week or so after the fist fight with Leroy in the cloakroom Sister Anne sent two of our classmates to the little mom and pop store across the street, (Jeffries) with a note. To our delight they came back with *Eskimo Pies* (ice cream on a stick) for each one of us. We giggled after school as we joked that when she went to confession for beating Leroy up the priest must have given her the penance of buying us all ice cream!

In her defense, she was old and tired and had wispy gray whiskers sticking out from her wimple. This and the fact that there were 50 children, some docile, some pranksters and some who had not yet had the grace of being diagnosed and medicated for ADHD added to her cross to bear.

Sister Mary Anne's comment and the sermon I heard the following Sunday sent me into a frenzy of wanting to save my father from the fires of Hell.

I am glad that some of the church's commands that we were taught in the '50s and early '60s have changed with the dictates of Vatican II and the latest Pope, Pope Francis.

CHAPTER EIGHT

Holy Water

The sermon I heard Sunday Morning soon after Sister Mary Anne's comments on who went to heaven and who went to hell, held my rapt attention. It was the story of a man possessed by a demon. He ranted, hollered, and threw anything he could grab as he screamed and wildly thrashed around. Jesus was the only one who could calm the man and cast out the evil spirit in him. As I listened, I prayed with tears stinging my eyes, "Please, God, help us all… stop my quivering and my tears before anyone sees me wiping away the evidence of my fear and sadness. Make my daddy stop drinking!"

We were taught that in case of impending death, we could baptize a person by pouring or sprinkling Holy Water and saying, "I baptize thee in the name of the Father and of The Son and The Holy Ghost." We also heard stories of St. Bernadette of Lourdes, France, and the miracles of healing that had been taking place since 1917. Very ill people still travel to the small town in France to be touched by the water where the Virgin Mary appeared to the young Bernadette, who was later canonized a Saint in 1933. I began to think that If I put holy water on Dad's side of the bed and prayed hard, maybe he would be filled with the Holy Spirit, and his drunken rages would stop.

What a naive young girl I was. I believed that my dad's contact with the Holy Water and my prayer would work a miracle; God's Grace would change him then and there.

Although I was afraid of him when he was drinking, he was still my daddy and sometimes he was lots of fun. I loved him and his sense of adventure and humor that made me laugh while working with him in his vegetable garden. He loved to go places and do fun things like ice skating or taking us to the park to swing and play on the monkey bars.

I prayed for him after he told me that he had never been baptized. I knew I couldn't force him to be baptized. I was only 7. I figured the reason he drank and went wild was because it was easy for the demons to overtake him because of his soul's unbaptized state. My childish mind surmised the devil made him drink, scream, rant and rave just like the sermon I heard about the evil demons possessing a man. While praying for him I thought of … what I thought was, a brilliant idea. It turned out to be not such a good idea, but my prayers for him to be baptized did become a reality twenty-five years later. God's timing is never our timing.

I often stopped at church to light a candle for my mom and dad on my way home from school. I loved the cool, calm quiet of the empty sanctuary. It seemed as though God heard my prayers when it was just the two of us in silence. As I learned from Thomas Keating, the originator of The Contemplative Prayer Movement in 1998, *"Silence is God's first language; everything else is a poor translation."* — Thomas Keating, *Invitation to Love: The Way of Christian Contemplation.*

The glowing red votive candles' mesmerizing flicker signaled to me that as long as that candle burned, God was hearing my pleas. The peace that descended on me felt as though

God had placed a warm blanket of love around my shoulders. It comforted, calmed and strengthened me to go back home.

We kept holy water in a font at home. I sometimes filled a little empty perfume bottle and brought some back home with me after school to replenish it when it had dried up. This time I took an empty Coca Cola bottle that Mom had put a sprinkling stopper on for when she dampened and ironed Daddy's work shirts. Saturday morning, I went to the church and filled it to the brim. I hoped and prayed that this would do the trick.

Behind the sacristy was the baptismal font where my little brother Mark and baby sister Jade had been baptized. There stood a large, gold, metal vat full of Holy Water that had been blessed by one of the priests.

It had a small spigot you could turn on and slowly and carefully drain some of the blessed water into a container to take home to be used when we made the sign of the cross and prayed.

I slowly turned the spigot, closely watching the blessed water as if looking away I might spill a drop which would be a sacrilegious act. The nuns encouraged us to have a Holy Water Font at home like the ones that were in the church as we entered into the sanctuary. Everyone dipped two fingers into the cool sacred water and made the sign of the cross, (forehead, sternum, left shoulder, and right shoulder) while saying, "In the name of the Father, and of the Son, and of the Holy Ghost." This was a prerequisite when entering the church to pray. My great idea was to sprinkle his side of the bed with the Holy Water. I believed this would do the trick!

Before my dad got home that day, I tiptoed into Mom and Dad's room and pulled back the blankets. I knew I would only have to do this once because we only needed to be baptized once. I doused the shape of a cross onto the crisp white sheets while praying, "I baptize thee in the name of The Father, and of The Son, and of the Holy Ghost." I pulled the blankets back up over the doused imprint of holy water in the shape of a cross and could hardly wait to see the results. I truly believed I would witness a miracle!

After saying my prayers and going to bed that night, I lay in a state of hopeful peace and drifted off to sleep with a smile on my face. I dreamed of ice skating down in the flats with Dad and laughing with Grannie over a cup of hot cocoa. I was awakened from my sweet dreams with the sound of my dad's deep booming voice shouting, "Who the hell peed in my bed?" My little brother sometimes peed the bed and I was terrified Dad would come into our room, yank him up from his sleep and beat the crap out of him. I knew if he came into our bedroom, I would have to tell him what I had done and he would beat the crap out of me instead. I shook quietly as I heard my mother talking in a hushed tone, "Shut up! If you wake the kids, we won't get any sleep at all tonight!" I was spared that night when I heard my dad grumbling and Mom shushing him while changing the sheets. That was my miracle!

CHAPTER NINE

Christmas Truth 1954

The city streets sparkled brightly with white, red and green twinkling lights; joyful Christmas Carols filled the air. The wonder and delight of the season stopped at our doorstep. The mood in our home was heavy and filled with an undercurrent of sadness, which sometimes still creeps up on me when I hear Christmas Carols until I remind myself of the many beautiful Christmases I have had with my husband, children and grandchildren. Living in this moment is the way to overcome the past.

I'm glad I found out at a tender age there is no Santa. The way it came to pass makes a good, laughable story at Christmas and made me appreciate the true beauty of the Birth of Love incarnate. The magical meaning of Christmas, its beauty and depth is the most important gift I received that year.

The reason for celebrating was Baby Jesus. I believed in Him and the Star of Bethlehem that led the Wisemen to the place he was born. Hearing the story that Mary and Joseph did not have much in the way of material possessions made me feel like I wasn't alone and it wasn't the most important thing in life. I just hated that it made my mother so very sad. It was sort of a relief when at the age of six I had Santa figured out as a game that parents played because of what I witnessed that Christmas Eve.

We lived in the upstairs apartment of our home in 1954. It wasn't until our parents and Grannie bought the house that we moved downstairs to the main floor. We didn't have a fireplace in the upstairs apartment. I was concerned that Santa would not know where we were when I heard that he came down the chimneys in homes of good little boys and girls

Dad explained that he would leave a window open next to the paper imprinted picture of a life-sized fireplace that he had purchased at Kresge's Five and Dime on Main Street. He stapled it onto the wall with his big industrial staple gun. He promised he would leave the window in the hallway ajar for Santa to come through. Santa would see my dad's big socks tacked onto the make-believe fireplace. Mom said that Santa would fill the stockings with oranges and candy and other sweet goodies.

Mom tried to get us to bed on Christmas Eve, but the excitement was more than we could hold in. We giggled and wiggled for quite a while as we wondered what Santa might bring. "What to my wondering eyes should appear, but a miniature sleigh, and eight tiny reindeer", is what Mom read from *The Night Before Christmas*. My six-year-old experience that evening was very different from the poem.

I fell asleep that Christmas Eve believing that Santa would find us. I awakened to noise on the roof above my bed. Clomp, Clomp, Clomp. Clomp, Clomp, Clomp. In my half-asleep, dreamy-minded state of confusion, I was sure that it was Santa's Reindeer on the rooftop above me! We had just learned the song, *Up on the Housetop* the week before in first grade. I was thrilled as only a six-year-old could be with knowing that Santa's Reindeer was at our house. Despite my excited anticipation I quietly slipped out of bed because I didn't want to awaken my sister and brother. They couldn't be quiet for anything. I was hoping to see Santa leaving colorful, exciting toys and gifts in brightly colored packages for all four of us.

I tiptoed down the hall and saw that Santa or the elves had filled each stocking tacked to the paper fireplace. Big, yummy red and white candy canes sticking out of each of my dad's big old socks let me know it was real! The excitement of getting a little peek at Santa in the living room was making my heart flutter!

I silently crept further and saw a green open mesh bag with oranges inside. A nearby box said *Six Candy Canes*, but there were only two in the box. Santa must have been in a hurry and not picked up his mess! Maybe the elves would tidy up on their way out.

I peeked into the living room and saw my mother, with a disgusted look on her face amidst green and red wrapping paper, scissors and tape. I ventured closer so that I could see clearly into the room now. and What to my wondering eyes appeared but my wooden-legged grandfather holding Dad's big Industrial Staple Gun and grinning ear to ear! Dad was struggling to get up from lying face down on the floor next to the coffee table cluttered with wrapping paper and empty Pabst Blue Ribbon Beer bottles. (Clomp, Clomp, Clomp). In Dad's drunken stupor, he couldn't figure out what the problem was! Grandpa had stapled Dad's Large, black and red plaid flannel shirt to our coffee table and he fell back down in a crumpled slurring mess each time he tried to get up! I did not see Santa! Merry Christmas!

The reindeer incident and the gifts we opened on Christmas Morning, no *Tiny Tears Doll* that I had requested in a letter to Santa, brought me to the realization that there was NO SANTA. It was confirmed by the look in my mom's sad eyes as we opened our presents — socks, coloring books, paper dolls and PJ's. on Christmas Morning.

The kids who lived downstairs opened up cowboy outfits, trucks, baby dolls that blinked their eyes and bicycles! Why? We behaved better than they did! They were always fighting with each other and getting paddled. So along with the realization that there was no Santa I realized that besides *Finding our Happy Places* we needed to realize that another of Mom's sayings was true: *life is not fair*.

Yes, that Christmas morning was a disappointment in so many ways. The worst part was the sad look on Mom's face and Dad's bleary-eyed headache. They were both so unhappy. Despite the beautiful tree with colorful lights and shimmering tinsel, the mood was very somber as Christmas Carols played in the background. I wished with all my heart that I could make them happy.

I was grateful that we had gone to Midnight Mass the night before. It was always the best part of Christmas and still is. The smell of incense and the beeswax candles combined with the organ playing softly and the choir singing *Gloria in Excelsis Deo* filled me with a deep peace as I received Communion.

We made tracks with our boots in the softly falling snow, awed by the moon reflecting and sparkling on icy snow drifts giving the appearance of tiny diamonds. It was the most beautiful and peaceful part of Christmas and it filled me with joy and hope for the New Year.

The four of us in front of Grandma's Christmas tree. Mom said the look on my face was due to my frustration after I said, "Hurry up and take the picture, they are all holding still!"

CHAPTER TEN

Bald-Headed Martha

Looking on the positive side; even though Santa did not bring me a *Tiny Tears Doll*, at least I still had my doll named Susan. My Susan's eyes were painted on so they stayed open all the time. Lill's doll, Martha, was a beautiful doll with long blonde hair. It *was* beautiful before Mark gave the doll a botched-up haircut. There were areas where it looked like she had a butch haircut and varying lengths of blonde tufts in other places. She seemed more real than my Susan, because when you laid her down her eyes shut as though she decided to take a nap. When you picked her up, her eyes opened. She even had eyelashes that swiped open and closed. Besides the botched-up hairdo, Martha had another unfortunate accident. We didn't know for sure how it happened. We assumed Mark, who loved to take things apart and examine the contents to see how things worked, had pried into Martha's remarkable eyes to see how they opened and closed.

Screeching like a banshee in the night Lill screamed and cried, "Eyes! EYES!" I shot into the room thinking she must be hurt. She sat cradling Martha in her lap crying, "Her eyes! Her eyes!" When I picked the doll up off Lill's lap, I could hear those eyes rattle around in the doll's empty cranium. It looked evil. It was scary seeing her eyes rolling around in her almost bald head. It made me recall stories people had told us about exorcisms by a priest on people possessed by demons.

I tried to check it out and saw that Martha's eye mechanism was flopping around far down in her head. Mark heard Lill's screams and figured he better fix it before Dad got home. He pulled Martha's head off of her neck, grabbed the eyeball mechanism with two fingers and shoved the eyes back into their proper resting place but they wouldn't stay put. He thought he had fixed it! It angered him that they would not stay in the eye sockets so he tossed the dolls head like a bowling ball down our long hallway. Lill and Jade watched in horror as *Bald-Headed Martha's* head went rolling past, blonde hair flying and eyeballs rattling.

After the initial shock, Mark and I started to snicker. We thought it was funny due to our sick sense of humor that we acquired from our mother. It became a new game to make us laugh and the torment began for Lill. We would hear Mark yell, "Here comes *Bald-Headed Martha,*" followed by the sight and sound of the doll's head, eyeballs clattering, rolling down the hallway! In time, Lill laughed too because we learned you could only cry for so long and then you had to laugh at the crazy in our lives; or go crazy!

Our childhood was unique! There were no snuggles, Rock a Bye Baby Lullabies, no hugs, no kissing the hurt to make it better. "Things are tough all over, get a grip," Mom would say if we whined or complained. No mushy stuff for us. Instead of *This little piggy went to market* or *You are my Sunshine,* Mom made up silly rhymes. While touching each of baby Jade's toes she quipped, "Big Toe, Hegnie Bo, Henny Whistle, Penny Whistle, Lum Bum." She also made up us silly limericks that made us laugh, but we couldn't repeat them. Dad used phrases like, "Blow it out your sea bag," and a lot of cursing words. Sailor talk, he called it. These and other sayings were from his Navy days. We knew better than to repeat them. Mom was very creative with her silly rhymes and little ditties that I learned at a very early age not to repeat any of these at my friends' houses.

If we complained about an injustice or heard of someone who was having trouble in their family, Mom's words of wisdom were. "That's life, everyone has their own crock of crap and we wallow in it as best we can." I decided I would not wallow if, and when, I fell into a crock of crap. I would crawl out! Grannie's words of wisdom were more positive in nature. "Cheer up, the Cherries will soon be ripe." She even said this in the winter when the trees were totally bare and dripping with frozen icicles. I knew it would be a long time before the cherries were ripe out in the back yard but I knew she meant, "Hang on, better times are coming." These words of wisdom from Grannie were from a song she remembered from 1908 when she was ten years old.

We learned to use our imaginations. We made up stories of talking birds, telling secrets to us and strange rhymes naming toes. We found humor, (sick or not) in whatever happened around us. We all share the trait of making light of unfortunate situations and finding any humor or positive thoughts we can to get us through hard times.

CHAPTER ELEVEN

Grannie

Grannie worked at a drug store on Ontario and Third Street in downtown Cleveland. In this century, she would be considered a Pharmacy Tech. There were no schools to get a certificate in dispensing prescribed medication back then. A degreed pharmacist would fill the orders and she would be at the store all day to give them to patients when they came in to pick them up. She took me to work with her in downtown Cleveland a couple of times and I watched her run back and forth between cosmetics and the drug department doing whatever needed to be done.

She loved both of the departments she worked in. She had a big red PDR (Physicians' Desk Reference) that she studied. I remember her showing me what the different colored and shaped pills were prescribed for. Grannie had a pill to cure everything: Colds, Coriciden, Stomach Aches, a minty flavored chewable called *Titralac,* or a big blue bottle of *Phillips Milk of Magnesia.*

For headaches she would give us *Aspirin.* She had a supply of *Darvon* for Mom's migraines and *Miltown* or *Phenobarbital f*or Mom and Dad's anxiety. She even gave us kids broken pieces of a little white pill to calm us down if she was near when Dad went into his rampages. It felt good to stop shaking inside. After I became an adult I wondered if she knew this was against the law?

When new hit records replaced the old tunes in the jukebox at the soda counter at her drug store, she brought home the old ones for us. We loved them! We sang and danced to these 45s (small vinyl records) that Grannie brought home from downtown Cleveland.

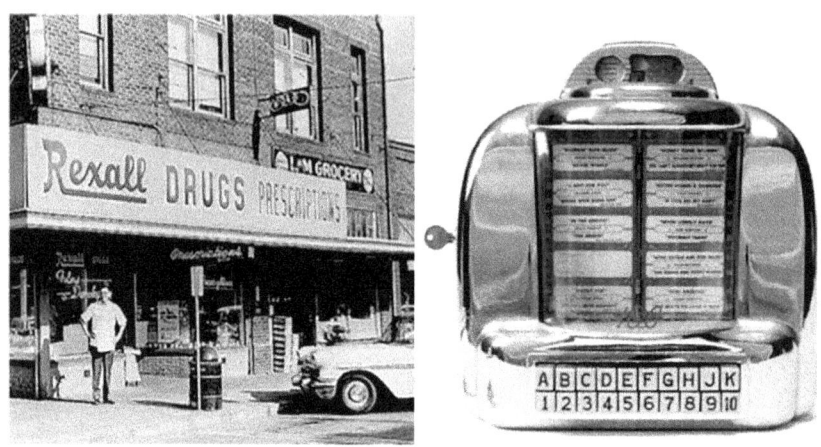

My brother especially loved listening to music and watching my sister and me dance our silly selves to exhaustion. He was three and had never uttered a single word. We tried to coax him, "Say Cookie, and I'll give you this cookie!" Say, *please*, and I'll take you for a ride in the wheelbarrow."

I could tell by the look on Mom's face that she was worried about him. He had fallen down 13 stairs when he was 2, and he blacked out. His eyes rolled back in his head just like *Bald-headed Martha's* had! We thought he was dead. Dad took him to the hospital, where they did an electroencephalogram, and the doctor said he was fine, so why didn't he talk? His response to us asking him to repeat a word we spoke to him was silence. It did not help. He would just stare at us or shake his head and run away.

One of the records Grannie brought home was *Oh My Papa*, sung by a '50s crooner, Eddie Fisher. The words told of a man who was missing his father. The day she brought that one home and put it on the record player, we heard my little brother start singing, "Oh My Papa" in a deep, monotone voice. He did not sing more than that one line, simply one verse, over and over, "Oh My Papa." He continued to sing it for months. When I think of it now, I wonder, *was it a plea or a prayer?*

CHAPTER TWELVE

Sauerkraut Angels

Every year, we ate Pork and Sauerkraut on New Year's Day. Grannie said it was a Polish/German tradition brought back from the Old Country that was supposed to bring good luck and lots of money in the new year. So far, it had not worked, but I looked forward to the yummy meal each year. It was a quiet day of watching the New York City *Macy's Day Parade* and working a puzzle on the dining room table after the dishes had been cleared and taken to the kitchen. All was calm. When things were calm and seemed good and quiet, I often had the uneasy feeling that it would not last long. Mom said it was "waiting for the other shoe to drop", she explained that to wait for the other shoe to drop meant to wait for an expected and inevitable event to occur. The event is most often negative. Even to this day that anxious feeling surfaces when things seem too good to be true.

In the middle of the that night, I awakened to loud voices and the crashing of things thrown in anger. Plates were hitting our dining room walls. Was it another nightmare, or was it real? Waking from a warm deep sleep to the sound of loud, angry voices jarred my senses. Fear shot from my stomach to my throat, like the time I stupidly stuck a bobby pin in an electrical outlet at the age of three because I thought it would light up; instead, I got jolted across the room and landed on my butt!

My impulse was to run, but to whom would I run? There was no one to run to. Where would I go? I could not leave Lill, Mark, and Jade. My racing heart and stomach-clenching spasms paralyzed me to be still. I whispered to my sisters and brother, "It's okay. Our angels are watching over us. We're okay; just pretend to be asleep." I lay praying that my parents would stop fighting so my heart and mind could calm down and we would be safe.

It had started again. It was calm when we went to bed, but it was inevitable to start again after two days of football and beer. No, it wasn't another nightmare. It was real. The loud crashing and angry cursing voices were in the next room. Jade pressed her little body tightly against me. She clenched my arm with her little hand. She was still, but wide-eyed. I smiled at her., "It's O.K. They will stop soon." Silently, I prayed they would.

Obscenities and threats were flying around the next room like bottle rockets on the fourth of July. Dad was screaming, "Fire! Fire!"

Mom was yelling out, "There is NO FIRE, you crazy drunk!"

Was there a fire? I had to know. I jumped out of bed and ran to the dining room to see if there were any flames in the kitchen where they were screaming at each other. There were no flames or smoke, but I did see my dad running around in his blue striped boxer shorts, waving his Japanese Bayonet in the air. It was a souvenir from WWII. He was threatening Mom not to come any closer to him. I also saw a plate of pork and sauerkraut that had been thrown onto the window seat where Lil had talked to the birds earlier in that day and I had etched icy angels.

Would this be like other times when they yelled and swore at each other and Dad would storm out for more beer. It was 3 a.m., and I knew the bars were closed. "By God, if you don't shut the hell up and leave me alone, I'll kill you and bury you in the backyard!" he bellowed. He continued to wave his souvenir from his tour of duty.

Mom was screaming, "Put that damn thing down and stop scaring the kids!"

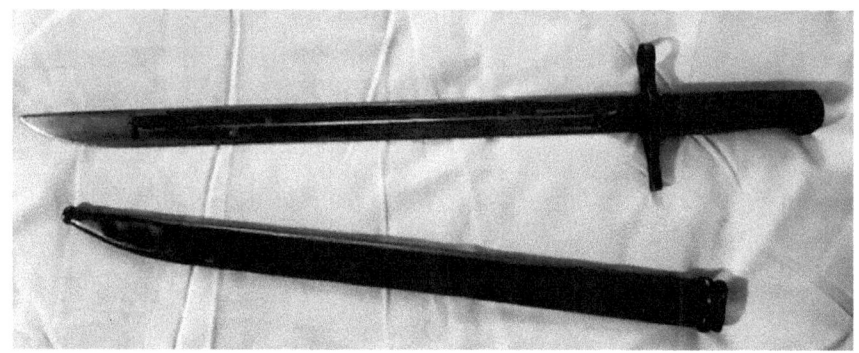

Should I gather the kids and hide in the closet again? No…we would be stuck there with no way to get out. Should I try to sneak my way to the phone and call the police? I went back into our bedroom to tell the kids there was no fire. Mark and Lill looked at me wide-eyed. I quietly said, "Put your shoes and coats on!" I grabbed a blanket to wrap around Jade and looked out into the dining room again. He was still waving the bayonet around and threatening to kill her.

Having tip-toed to the phone on the window seat, I dialed the numbers for the police department that Mom had written on the back of the phonebook. He saw me on the phone giving our address to the police and lunged towards me. Grabbing the phone, he pulled it out from the wall.

I bolted to the bedroom, picked up Jade, and told Mark and Lill to follow me quickly. We ran down the front porch steps through the snow and down to the big oak tree out front. I yelled to Mom as we went out the front door, begging her to follow us. "Get out of there, Mom! The door is open."

She was 5'2", and he was 6'2." I never understood why she would fight with him. Although he spanked us with his hand or belt, I had never seen him hit her, but when she clobbered him with her blue, hob-nailed ashtray and drew blood I thought for sure he was going to kill her by the angry, crazed look on his face.

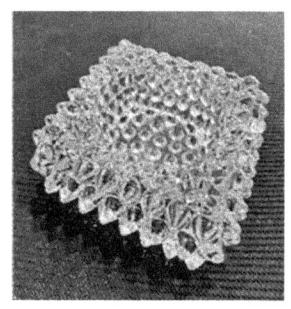

I watched from a distance on the sidewalk a few minutes later as two policemen took my dad down to the floor and handcuffed him. After they got Dad into the patrol car, one of the officers came up to us as we hid behind our big oak tree and took us back inside. I was grateful and humiliated and hoped that none of the neighbors had seen what happened.

CHAPTER THIRTEEN

The Calm After the Storm

As daybreak illuminated my bedroom the next morning, I could see that snow was gently floating like cherry blossoms in a soft caress of breeze. I quietly walked into the other room to see if Mom was awake or asleep. The sun was shining through the glass of the window panes where the pork and sauerkraut had been thrown in a rage the night before. Sauerkraut was stuck to the glass in places giving my ice angels the look of blonde, albeit very smelly hair.

Mom was drinking coffee in the kitchen and puffing on her cigarette with a very ill-tempered look on her face and I knew not to say anything to her. I needed to be alone. I needed to breathe fresh air. Being outside on a cold winter day when the house was all closed up cleared my smoke-filled nose and lungs. I needed to breathe deep and feel peace and calm.

I put my boots and coat on, found my gloves and scarf and told her I was going to walk in the snow for a bit. I decided to walk up the block to church and light a candle. As I knelt there in the silence I started to cry. I wanted to talk to someone. I had been talking to God last night and this morning and I wasn't hearing any answers. Either I wasn't hearing HIM or he wasn't listening to me! Who could I talk to? Whom could I trust? We had relatives that lived an hour away and although I knew their names, I didn't know their phone numbers. Mom would kill me if I said anything to anyone and a long-distance call would be expensive. Besides that, Dad had pulled the phone out of the wall last night and I didn't have any money for the phone in the phone booth on the corner of Erie and State Street. Even if I did call a relative, what could they do anyway? We had not seen any of them for a couple of years. Mom said it was because of Dad and his drinking. I felt totally alone and hopeless.

An idea came to me to go and talk with one of the priests. It wouldn't be for a confession, more like asking for advice. It would be a request for any help they could give at all and lots of prayers. Maybe God would hear a priest pray about our situation? Maybe God put the idea in my head to talk with a priest. In the midst of feeling lost and afraid a tiny spark of hope nudged me to the rectory.

Walking up the brick steps I took a deep breath and rang the bell. The door opened slowly. The housekeeper, Mrs. O'Leary said, "Can I help you?' "May I please speak with one of the priests?" She didn't ask me to come in but smiled and said, "Just a minute, I'll see if he can see you." Father Sidley came to the door, looked at me quizzically and said, "Yes?"

I stammered, "I need to talk with someone because I am afraid my father is going to hurt us when he is drunk. He threatened my mom last night and I don't know what to do." He frowned at me and said, "Well first of all, you need to pray about it. Go home, put a skirt on. It's disrespectful for you to come to the rectory or to church dressed in slacks. When you have changed your clothes, come back to the church and kneel and pray." With that…he mumbled something about being busy with other things and he slowly closed the door.

Humiliated and angry, I wondered what difference did it make if I had a skirt or slacks on? It was cold out here! Our navy-blue jumpers and white blouse uniforms were to be worn to school. Dresses and hats or scarves were to be worn to church, but I never heard anything about what we should wear to the rectory. Sometimes If I didn't have a scarf with me I had even put a stupid Kleenex on my head when I went into the church so I didn't break the rule about wearing something on your head when entering the sanctuary. I tried to always follow the rules, even the stupid ones that I didn't understand!

I know I asked too many questions. Questions like, "What happened to the people who might be in Purgatory for eating meat on Friday?" "What good did it do for them to be in Purgatory in the first place?" "Did they open the gate and let them out and say, 'Not a problem anymore, go on through the Pearly Gates we changed the rules with Vatican II and its' no longer a sin!'" "Why was it a sin to begin with?"

I never ate meat on Friday. I was a rule follower but my searching, questioning mind tried to find answers to question that had no answers that anyone could give me. Later, as a teenager, I read *Live the Questions Now* by Ranier Maria Rilke, 1903. His quote, "Live the questions now. Perhaps then, someday far in the future, you will gradually, without even noticing it, live your way into the answer." As I read it, I hoped it was true. Someday maybe I would understand many things that right now were incomprehensible to me. This bit of wisdom did come to pass in my later years.

I was not going home to change. I had already prayed about it. I was angry. Something inside of me felt stronger, rebellious even! I had to walk my anger out. I walked in the snow for an hour in the big open field beyond our backyard. I often wandered around that field when I needed to be alone, to think, to pray. I crossed over the field onto the brick road where the Depot Café and the New York Central Train Depot stood. I often would meet Grannie coming off the train from work there or sometimes sneak over to see if my dad's car was parked at the Depot Café when he didn't come home. When my knees and feet began to feel numb, I decided to go home.

I came in the back door and took off my boots. It would take a while for my toes to stop stinging and burning as they warmed up. The kids were watching cartoons and Mom was still drinking coffee and smoking another cigarette.

"Grannie wants you to go with her."

"Are we taking a cab to the A & P?" I asked.

"No, she is going to make bail for your dad and get him out of jail."

I couldn't believe it! How could she do that? As nicely as I could, I said, "I don't want to go."

Mom snapped back, "Well, Grannie doesn't want to walk all the way there by herself. You are the oldest. She needs you." I wondered silently why Mom didn't go with her instead of sending me.

My mind started whirling. What if one of my friends from school saw me going into the police station and coming out with my dad? Mom was right, though, Grannie needed me. The sidewalks were icy and Grannie was old. She occasionally had bouts of vertigo and I didn't want her to fall and break a bone on the ice! I knew I should go with her but I didn't want to. I told Grannie I didn't want to go because I was afraid. I knew Dad would be mad at me for calling the police and I did not want anyone to see me coming out of the Police Station with my dad. She promised me that after we gave them the money for bail, we would walk right out and we wouldn't see Dad there. "I will take you down the street for a hot chocolate at the counter at Kresges and then we will stop at the library on the way back to get you a couple of books to read."

I decided the chances of seeing a school friend early on a Christmas Vacation morning in the snow were slim so we started on the five-block trek to the Police Station. We entered a side door and went into an office. It was a relief to get out of the bitter wind. Grannie gave them my dad's name, handed them the cash and got a receipt. She thanked the police lady, and we walked out down the street to Kresges Five and Dime. My hot chocolate was topped with a massive amount of whipped cream. The day was bitter cold, but the hot chocolate was sweet and warm.

The Mystery of Mom

I find solace in this misty, gray day. It is the tenth anniversary of my mother's passing into peace. I am tearful thinking of the hard time we had connecting. Despite the tears and regrets accompanying this misty morning, I find a profound sense of peace. I take comfort in knowing I did everything within my power for Mom. I have come to terms with the pain, the regret, and the confusion that plagued our relationship for so many years.

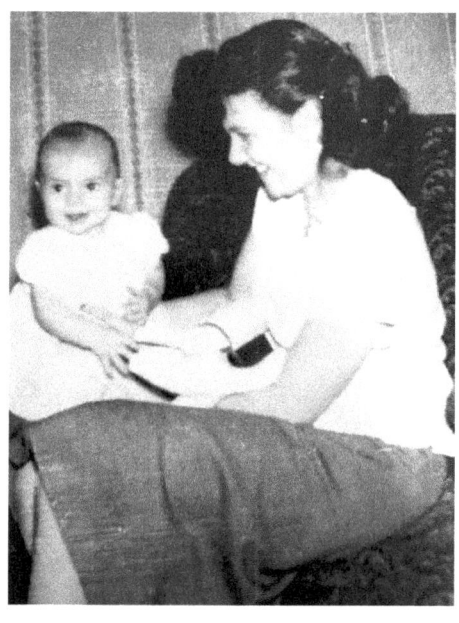

Until recently, I was still mentally beating myself up for not being able to help her. The manipulative hold she had perfected when she was alive worked long after she passed through this life onto the next. A therapist I saw for a short time surmised that Mom sounded like a Borderline Personality who leaned on me as her confidant. Mom told me things no child should have to assimilate.

Being placed in the role of an adult friend is a heavy burden for a child. I didn't have the coping skills or life experience to know what to say or do when she took me into her confidence.

When I was five, I watched her take cellophane tape and run it over my daddy's jacket. I had never seen her do that before. I was curious. Mommy was crying as she told me, "See! See these blonde hairs on your daddy's jacket? What color is mommy's hair?"

"It's brown like mine, Mommy."

"This is not my hair. I do not have blonde hair! Your daddy is running around with a blonde woman!" It made me sad to see tears running down her face and hear her cry as she continued to run that tape over the shoulders and down the front of that brown tweed jacket.

I felt helpless. How could I make my mommy feel better? I tried to hug her, but she jerked away and cried more. I could not comfort her, and I didn't understand why Daddy would "run around!" Was he playing tag?

Many years later, when they were fighting and hurling accusations at each other, the memory came to me, and I understood that she thought he had been with other women as early as eight years before. Dad swore it was a false accusation.

Mom was a mystery to me during my childhood and teenage years. When I was very young, there was a sweet, caring tenderness in her eyes when she looked at me, making me feel loved and wanted. On a good day, she loved us in her own way, with a wink or a smile. She was not a mother who lavished us with hugs and loving words, but we knew we were loved.

Then there was the other side. We never knew which side would be prevalent at any given moment. It was a wild and continual roller coaster of intense emotion, crazy fun and laughter, or deep depression and anger. Mom had many facets: the soft, kind-eyed, sad side that made me ache for her and the other side: "Toughen Up! I don't want to hear your complaints." "Grow Up." "Get over it; things are tough all over." "Don't be so damned dramatic." "I can't wait until you are all grown and I can live my life." I did everything possible to please Mom and make her happy, but it never worked.

The door to a comfortable, loving relationship was slammed shut when I was 17, and Mom told me, "Get the Hell out and don't come back!" I did leave and went to live with a high school friend, but I went back many times to visit. I called her regularly and sent her cards and notes. I tried to heal our relationship even though there were years I was told, "Mom doesn't want to talk to you."

Finally, when she was in her late 80s, we had a few years when a more loving connection came to be, and it was that way until her death at the age of 90.

Remembering the stories she told us about her childhood, I understand how she learned to be tough and thought our problems were minimal and not worth mentioning. She always laughed when she told us stories of her childhood. She insisted she had great adventures as a child from age six to twelve during the Great Depression, traveling in boxcars with hobos and going days without food.

She was frightened when she and her parents hopped onto freight trains and found shady-looking hobos in the same train car sitting across from them. They jumped into railroad cars that were dark, dirty, and sweaty-smelling. The malodorous smell mixed with something else was sickening. She said that once, her dad accepted a mason jar filled with something from one of the filthy men. "He wouldn't let me have a sip, even though I was thirsty. After he chugged it down and I smelled the residue on his breath, I knew it was liquor." She had smelled that on his breath many times before. She added, "It was probably Moonshine, because it was during prohibition."

One night, a hobo shared his meal with her. They ate stale bread smeared with bacon grease! She said it was delicious because she had not eaten in two days.

They walked so many miles looking for a job and a place to live that Grandpa George's shoes had holes in the soles, so he reinforced them with cardboard he found lying on the roadside.

She remembered the horror of finding a man lying in the weeds on the side of the road when she was seven. She stayed with her mom, Julia, while her dad, George, went to see if the man in the ditch was OK.

She said Grandpa George returned with a dazed stare, shaking his head. "That poor guy has been dead for a while." He smiled as he pointed to the newly acquired shoes on his feet. "He won't be needing these where he is going!"

Mom and her parents waited patiently in food lines to receive something to eat. They stopped at church rectories, asking for help. She told us there were symbols scratched in the dirt or on a sidewalk to give those who needed it a clue about where they might find a meal. A sketch of a cat meant a kind woman lived there. A circle with an X in the middle said they would be given some food at this place. A cross signaled if you talked about religion, they would take pity and provide you with food instead of shooing you away or telling you to move on.

She told us her earliest Christmas memory with a smile on her face. Grandpa George had started a new job at a butcher shop, and Grannie Julia took in mending and sewing. This income enabled them to rent a room in a boarding house in Waukegan, Illinois, and enroll her in first grade at a nearby school.

Their room was up a flight of creaky steps that announced when someone came down from the second or third floor to eat one of the meals included in their room and board fee. It was warm and clean, and the best part was the little Christmas tree set up in the entryway.

While eating dinner—soup and bread with other roomers—at the dining room table, they heard the joyous singing of "Jingle Bells" coming from the front porch. They all got up and looked out the front door to see a group singing "Joy to the World" and "We Wish You a Merry Christmas" in the snowy darkness.

As the group started to walk away, a woman came up the porch steps and handed her a little black stuffed dog made of oilcloth material. "Merry Christmas, little girl," she said with a smile. Mom remembered that the little black dog had hand-stitched shoe button eyes and a red ribbon tied around its neck. This was her first Christmas present at the age of six, and she was thrilled!

Not long after Christmas, Grandpa lost his job again, and when they needed money to pay for the last two months' room and board, they couldn't pay. Her dad carried her down those creaky steps, hoping no one would hear them, and they left in the middle of the night to hop on another train for another new adventure.

She always laughed when we exclaimed with shock or concern as she told us stories of her childhood. She insisted she had great adventures from the age of six to eleven during the Great Depression.

Despite her denial, I know she was deeply hurt by her father's alcoholism and the hard times she experienced as a child. Always being the "new" kid as they jumped from town to town was tough for her introverted self. It worsened the situation that her father had trouble keeping a job due to his alcoholism, so they often picked up and moved when rent on a room was due, and there was no money to pay for it.

She loved dogs. They were always her closest friends. A dog would always befriend her, no matter where they went. Dogs were her companions because she was extremely introverted. Since dogs can sense people's emotions, they may have felt her need for companionship and comfort.

She and her parents frequently moved to new cities, so she didn't have time to make friends with kids her age. It was easier to talk to dogs and pet their warm, furry heads. Building a friendship with a dog was much easier for her and better than talking to people. The dogs' wagging tails and wet, sloppy kisses made her feel accepted and loved despite her shy, introverted nature.

It is easy to understand how a child's formative years filled with drunkenness, insecurity and loneliness would lead to trust issues and cause a person to build a wall around their heart and soul to protect them from further feelings of insecurity and anxiety. As an adult, remembering these stories that she told us of her childhood helped me make sense of the mystery of Mom.

CHAPTER FOURTEEN

PTSD

In May of 2000, it became clear to me that Dad's alcoholism was partially due to *Post-Traumatic Stress Syndrome*. After WWII the condition was called *Shell Shock*. This condition, afflicting thousands of veterans suffering from nightmares and flashbacks after the Vietnam War, brought the term Post-Traumatic Stress *Syndrome* into conversations in the 60s and '70s. In June of 2000 we were able to understand that his alcoholism and the drug abuse that plagued our family was partially due to PTSD.

When I visited Dad in the hospital the month before he died, I put the pieces of his trauma together and saw how it manifested in his struggle for sobriety. I had left home broken and confused more than 35 years earlier. Why did my family experience constant trauma and dysfunctional pain? I realized the answer the very last time I saw him alive while visiting him in the hospital.

He kept groaning that a fire was burning in the corner of his hospital room. Horrified, he believed it was real. Of course, there was no fire, but he thought it was real. He believed flames would engulf the room, and begged me to run and save myself. "Get out! Get out, save yourself!"

A stroke had taken his speech to an almost unintelligible slur. His bushy black and white eyebrows wildly rose and fell as he explained what he saw in the corner.

"Fire! Fire! Get out!" I wondered why he was so terrified! Why fire? In my conversation with Mom later, she speculated that he saw the fires of hell where God was sending him. There was, of course, no actual fire over there in the corner. Then a faint memory flickered.

Seeing how terrified he was by a non-existent fire made me recall the story Dad told me years before. He disclosed his experience of being on the USS *St. George's* deck in the Pacific in 1945. He said he heard the alert that an incoming Japanese Fighter Plane was approaching. Because of the warning, many of the guys were aware and began to take cover.

I can still hear Dad's stern, booming voice exclaiming, "Hell, you can't escape a Kamikaze plane! The whole area where the plane crashed into the ship lit up in a fiery explosion. Three men were killed instantly. As a Pharmacist Mate, I was to run and shoot morphine into my screaming crewmates severely injured and burned bodies." He told how a seaplane crane had come crashing down on one man holding him fast under the wreckage that had broken loose in the crash. The rescue workers could not get near enough to him due to the intense heat. All hands on deck were horrified at the screams. "Sometimes I drink to blackout, so I can't hear Bill screaming anymore."

USS St. George

Under Attack By Japanese Aircraft

During one of the frequent air raids in the Pacific the ship's gunners shot down an enemy plane on 29 April. A week later the USS St. George was hit by a kamikaze. Thanks to a warning from Louis (Jack) Norvelle Tickle, an airplane mechanic who had been on deck at the time and was able to spot the Japanese before they hit, only three men were killed. Unfortunately, the ship's seaplane crane was destroyed. Nevertheless, the tender remained on station, using a barge crane to lift seaplanes for repairs; and, in addition, provided repair support to destroyers and destroyer escorts." (https://en.wikipedia.org/wiki/USS_St.George_(AV-16)

Seeing how agitated he was by the fire he believed would harm me, I turned on the faucet in the nearby sink and reassured him that the fire was being extinguished. I placed my hand on his bony, rigid shoulder. I felt his taut muscles relax as the sound of running water calmed him. "Do you remember taking me down to the river at Recreation Park in the summer?" "Remember how you tried to teach me to skip stones in the river when we gathered rocks for your rock garden in our front yard? I never did get the hang of it!" I continued, "I remember those little white flowers that we planted in between the rocks that still come up every spring. Do you remember those little flowers? Think of planting those little flowers in our garden and being down at the river with me.

"I love you Dad and God loves you; just relax, God has put the fire out for good."

He smiled and slurred, "I love you, remember that and don't remember anything else." The tension flowed from his body like the water draining into the sink. He relaxed and fell asleep.

Leaving his room, I walked down the hospital corridor sobbing uncontrollably and made my way to the dark parking lot. Regret surged up in sobs over and over. I felt unbearable grief for what we all had experienced and what might have been. I was devastated by the pain that the whole family had lived with for so many years. My sorrow, combined with a deep-seated volcanic anger that I had been trying to control, pushed down, and held in for over 40 years, turned into a furious rage with myself.

Was I stupid for still caring for him? What kind of an idiot loves a father who terrorized her as a child? Why did I care about him at all? Why did I want to ease his pain? Why did I tell him that he had been a good dad because he had made me strong? Well, he had made me strong, because as the saying goes, *"What doesn't kill you makes you stronger."*

I knew it would be the last time I saw him alive. I could not let my anger consume me, I had to let it go. He would be gone soon, and this anger would only hurt me and my pain would continue.

He loved his country. He loved us as best he could despite the trauma that haunted him. After losing most of his family, his home and his business due to alcoholism, he joined AA in his later years and learned to fly sober and high. He rose above his problems and soared on the Power of God, like a Gooney Bird.

CHAPTER FIFTEEN

June 26, 2000

An 8:20 a.m. shock! If only we had left one day earlier. We were packed up and ready to go tomorrow to be with him one last time, and we didn't make it before he died.

I feel hollow and empty at my core, as though I am walking with a big hole through my middle, like a cartoon character who has been shot, dead center, with cannon ball. I am weak-kneed and fuzzy-headed, as though the breeze could blow right through me and topple me over. Nothing seems real.

I'm glad I made the trip to see him in May when I first heard he was hospitalized. We knew he had a stroke but he was stable and not in ICU. I knew he was ill but didn't know death was so close. I was so sure I would be able to see him again when we went back home in late June and early July for two weeks.

I don't want to go through this today, July 3, 2000. I want to skip to tomorrow and have this all be a memory, like a bad dream. We woke up in the hotel room at 6:00 a.m. after having driven twelve hours the day before. We only had five hours sleep last night. Now, on we go to the Memorial Service. My body aches from yesterday's long car ride, and my heart aches with many memories and the sadness of him being gone before we made it home.

We were the first to arrive at the church. It was a small wooden framed building of 1950s vintage painted a dull and melancholy gray.

Very narrow stained-glass windows accompanied fifteen pews on either side of the sanctuary. The windows glinted bright colors with a bit of sun that filtered through huge canopies of leaves on the trees around the church. The giant trees engulfed the slate roof and obscured the bell tower. It was my first time being in a Lutheran Church. The Pastor, Rev. Fitzpatrick, had known my father for 20 years and welcomed us as we came in. I told him I was Chuck's daughter by his first marriage. He seemed surprised and said he didn't realize he had children.

I didn't know the similarities and shared beliefs between Catholics, Episcopalians and Lutherans. As I looked through a prayer book in the pew, the words were very familiar, and my father had taken them on as his own in his 50th decade.

I felt comforted after talking with the pastor that Dad had been happy. He loved his church and was overjoyed on his baptismal day some 20 years before. He received the last rites of the church the day before he died. I remembered the Holy Water I had doused onto his bed and was grateful that God had answered my childhood prayers. Miracles happen in God's own way, in God's own time.

His wife, Irene, planned the service as soon as possible. She wanted it that way because she was exhausted and grief-stricken. She planned to leave town right after the service and move in with her daughter; the quicker, the better.

Knowing Dad's love for the Navy, Mark wanted to have the tribute of a Twenty-one-gun salute, and taps played to end the service. There was hardly any time to arrange it. Irene had refused to hear of it initially and didn't want it done for some reason. Her daughter, Gerry, convinced her mother the day before the service that Dad likely wanted to have the honor since he loved the Navy. Gerry arranged to have the VFW present and perform the recognition of a salute by the VFW. Mark told me how happy he was to know he would receive Dad's flag at the ceremony.

The VFW men arrived. Sergeant Robinson spoke with the Rev. Fitzpatrick in the hallway outside the sanctuary. I overheard as he explained how the flag was to be presented. The reception order was the 1st wife, then the oldest son, and down the line. Irene quickly announced that she wanted the flag given to her as she was his wife. Sergeant Robinson agreed with her instructions, not realizing she was Dad's second wife. She and her family walked away and sat down in the first pew.

As Irene left, Mark approached the man from the VFW. I got up and stood with my brother. Sergent Robinson explained the order of presentation to him. Mark said, "I am the only son. My mother was his first wife."

The sergeant said, "Oh, I thought *she* was the first wife!"

Mark looked confused and I chimed in, "No, she is his second wife; Mark is his only son."

Robinson was shaken because he had just told Irene he would present the flag to her. As the music in the sanctuary started to play, he said, "Just tell me who to give it to."

Mark responded, "I'll go talk to Irene and explain."

After Mark walked away, I told the sergeant, "Give it to his son. That is what Dad would have wanted."

Mark approached Irene and explained that she was the second wife and the order of presentation was first wife and then the first or only son. Her reply was angry… "Not now, Mark, they are giving it to me. I can't deal with this now. It is decided!"

I watched as Mark stood rigidly with a hot and angry glare. Veins stood at attention in his neck, pulsing adrenaline to his muscles. He was rigid, trying to control the urge to go for her throat! He was the image of our dad at his angriest. It was easy to imagine that he might go for her throat or pummel her right now in front of God and everyone who cared enough to come to this Memorial Service.

I can't change this. Dad was dead, and our grief was overshadowed by the aching regret over what could have been and never was. I tried to let it go, repeating, *All is Well,* a Julian of Norwich quote and *God is in Control*, Romans 8:28. Without making a scene, we have no choice but accept that she would be getting the flag.

The litany of accepting the inevitable played over and over in my mind as my heart ached for Mark, who thought he'd be receiving his father's flag. Now, she would have it. She had our dad, and now the final coup; she will have his flag also, even though she never paid the price it cost us in fear of his drunken rages.

Sergeant Robinson was waiting with me at the back of the center aisle for Mark's cue as to what to do. As I watched Irene and Mark a few pews ahead of me, the sergeant was rambling on about the rightful presentation of the flag. He said he would not have agreed to give it to her if he had known she was not the first wife! Now, what should he do? He didn't want to cause trouble.

The service was starting. Robinson said through clenched teeth, "Just tell me who to give it to. Who should I give it to?"

I looked at him and said, "Give it to Mark!"

I took my place between my husband and sister. The flag was rightfully Mark's. How could she keep it for herself and prevent him from having his father's flag?

My brother walked slowly, controlling his anger, fists clenched at his sides, jaw firmly set. Mark sat down beside his wife, Terri, in the third pew in front of my husband and me. Terri put her arm around his shoulder, leaned close, and whispered, "There is nothing you can do. Try to relax."

I listened to the eulogy about a man who came into his spirituality late in life. Father Fitzpatrick told how happy and excited Dad had been to be baptized at the age of 52. He had helped many younger men in their quest for sobriety through AA at the church. He was a great help to a family with a grown son severely handicapped with Cerebral Palsy. Dad stayed at the house with this disabled young man when the parents wanted a relaxing weekend alone. They didn't worry because their son was well taken care of by a guy who had been a male nurse in WWII. He was a good man who loved the outdoors. He was artistic, loved music, and played the cello in high school. Despite his WWII trauma, he had turned himself around toward the end of his life.

Dad wasn't able to give us much of anything as children. We received neither time, money, support, or understanding as we struggled to grow up. We feared him, sometimes hated him, and sometimes loved him. He was our father, and in rare moments, we could see a glimmer of loving-kindness and a joking guy who loved having a good time.

His Honorable Discharge from the Navy symbolized that he had done something we could be proud of. It was something he was able to do well and finish with honor. I had been happy that Mark would have Dad's flag as a symbol of Dad's ability to do something good, right and honorable. Mark needed a symbol of his father's courage, love, and determination to overcome the pitfalls of his own life and now he would not have it. It was going to Irene.

The Honor Guards filed slowly to the altar where a 1945 photo of Dad in his Navy Attire was displayed next to his ashes. They saluted one by one. It was a slow deliberate heartfelt snap to the brown in direct opposition to my anxious racing heart. The Navy Hymn, "Eternal Father Strong to Save" floated from the organ through the sanctuary as we processed out of the church to witness the 21 Gun Salute and presentation of the flag.

My last directive to Robinson was to give the flag to Mark and now I was fearful that if he did give it to Mark instead of Irene there might be a scene since she was so adamant that it was rightly hers.

The 1945 photo of Dad in his Navy attire that was displayed next to his ashes and saluted by the Honor Guard at his memorial service.

I looked at Robinson and his eyes were closed! Was he praying or was he afraid to present the flag because of the confusion. Maybe he sensed that all hell was about to break loose! Slowly he opened his eyes and gave the flag to Irene. I felt my heart would explode with anger and overwhelming sadness. She had Dad and now she had his flag.

I was biting my lip and trying to breathe when I heard Irene say, "Mark, this was your father's. He would have wanted you to have it".

Dad loved his country and tried to love us the best he could despite the trauma that haunted him. After losing most of his family, his home, and his business due to alcoholism, he joined AA in his later years and learned to fly high while sober. He rose above his problems and soared on the power of God, like a Gooney Bird.

CHAPTER SIXTEEN

Bird or Angel, 1980

Memories surface unbidden like mist rising from a cool rain on hot summer roads. Triggered by a particular smell, sound, or how light breaks through a windowpane on a winter day, the past comes alive again. The recollection of the day Lill sat on the window seat twenty-four years earlier talking to birds as the wind blew flurries of white in wintry blasts came to me because it was a frigid, snowy day. I had been rocking in my chair, wrapped in a blanket, depressed and anxious. I was crying and staring out the window, watching the birds eat at the feeder, and praying that God would ease my hyperventilating breath, palpitations and missed heart beats. I needed to calm down.

It made me smile a little, remembering my little sisters as cute red-haired cherubs and my sweet dark-haired brother singing his three-word song, *Oh My Papa*. They were all under the age of 5 at the time. I also recalled how it felt then as an eight-year-old. I was a child with no childhood. I lived as a miniature adult, trying to make sense of the chaos of my family. How do children deal with the lunacy of living in an alcoholic and drug-addictive hell? How do children cope and find some way to deal with the chaos? Do they fantasize, like Lill? Do they turn inward and refuse to talk, like Mark? Or, do they shove it down and suppress all memories, like Jade?

I chose to believe I could change things in some way. I prayed for and hoped that circumstances would get better. It would improve if I prayed hard enough, behaved for my parents, and helped them as much as possible. There had to be something I could do; something to fix it! This attitude of needing to be in control, ease others' pain, and improve all the imperfections around me set up an impossible life script for me to follow.

I longed as an eight-year-old to take the pain away from all of them. I still had nightmares and night terrors of trying to gather Lill, Mark and Jade to the cellar doors and down the stairwell to safety as a whirling tornado was touching down in our back yard. It was just like a scene from The Wizard of Oz when I dreamed this. Should I keep trying to save them or just save myself? Until recently I thought I had failed them all because I left home at 17 after Mom told me to "Get the Hell out and don't come back." Now, so many years later I felt I was failing my husband and daughters.

I knew I was just a child back then and had no control over the situation, but I kept praying and trying to control what I could. I promised myself that the kind of family I wished for would be a reality someday. When I was all grown up, I could make it perfect. I would make sure it was the way it should be. Thinking this way was how I made it through my childhood. I believed with all my heart that my adult life would be perfect. I projected myself into the future and just had to hang on until then.

Now, 24 years later, depressed and filled with anxiety, I sat, trying to calm myself wrapped in a blanket of baby blue. Rocking, breathing, rocking, breathing. The anxiety attacks, physical pain, and phobias were extreme. I was a prisoner in my home. I was trapped by fear. I could not go to the grocery store alone and I was even unable to walk to the mailbox by the road without an anxiety attack. I hated myself for not being the perfect wife and mother I had promised myself so many years ago that I would be. I needed to control, to make everything wonderful; it was obsessive. I wanted to make life perfect for my husband and children because I loved them so much and felt they deserved better than me. Our life was not the way I had planned it because I couldn't rid myself of the depression, pain, and missed heartbeats and the tightness in my chest that made me hyperventilate and feel as though my heart would explode.

Deep in my psyche I longed for death. I was losing it and wanting the pain to be over. It seemed the only way to escape the physical pain and emotional terror and give my husband and beautiful daughters a better life was by giving them a life without me. Sleep gave me no relief. I was tired of the nightmares of running and hiding from someone or something wanting to hurt my children and me. I would awaken screaming and gasping for air. My husband would grab me, hold me, and gently waken me with, "It's just a dream, I am here, you are OK."

My husband saw me smiling as we drove through the countryside on a gray February day. "I'd almost forgotten how pretty you are when you smile. Why are you so happy?"

I looked at him, smiled again, and said, "Oh, it is just so peaceful out there," while motioning to the cold, gray tombstones in a cemetery we were passing. "None of them are in pain anymore."

Begging God for help, I prayed for release from my panic and depression. I needed someone to help me desperately. It seemed no one knew what to do or say to ease my body, mind, or soul. Dr. Smith insisted I continue to take the Valium he prescribed. I did not want to take them but they did work for a short time. Now I seemed to need to take them more than every four hours. Anxiously awaiting until it was time for the next dosage, I alternately paced the floor around the room or rocked back and forth reading Psalm 62, "My soul finds rest in God alone." (NIV), as tears slowly welled up and ran down my cheeks.

I tried concentrating on what my husband had told me before taking the children to school and preschool and going to work: "You are not a failure! You are a good wife and mother, and I promise you will get well. You are just having a horrible time this winter. Just stay warm and take care of yourself. I love you."

As I cried and prayed and rocked back and forth, another panic attack overwhelmed me. The familiar tingly numbness spread over my face, arms, and legs as my heart pounded fast and furious. The sensation of smothering for lack of air was causing me to breathe more rapidly, making me feel totally out of control. Angry with myself for being so crazy and not getting a grip on my emotions I was overwhelmed with hatred for myself and longing for relief. I decided to take another pill a little early. How many had I taken three hours ago? Could I take two more? The thought crossed my mind to take the whole damn bottle of Valium that the doctor prescribed and end it all. I could not bear the thought of leaving a legacy of a mother who committed suicide for my daughters but the longing for peace tormented me.

As I opened the bottle of pills, a bird flew over my head and hit the window. It bounced off, stunned, and landed on the floor. Hearing feathered wings flapping and fluttering overhead made me put the bottle down. Freaking out, I wondered if I had gone over the edge and was hallucinating! Was there a bird in my bedroom? How did it get in? The house was locked up tight. Everyone in this small Ohio town in the Snow Belt had sturdy storm windows in place this time of year. My husband kept the fireplace flue shut tight to keep the winter wind from blowing into the house. This bird was really here in my room! It was frantically trying to find a way out by continually battering its small, feathered frame into the window glass until it hit the floor and was still.

Seeing a bird in my bedroom in the dead of winter was a shock. It took my mind off the smothering, tingling sensation for a moment as compassion for a helpless creature riveted my attention.

I spoke to it gently, "You poor little thing! How did you come to be trapped here? Be Still. Calm down. I know you are trying to find a way out to the light, but banging your head against the walls and windows will not help you escape. You are only hurting yourself. You cannot find your way out alone. Let me help you! Stop trying so hard! Stop beating yourself up! The harder you try to free yourself, the more you hurt yourself. Please trust me. Let me help you."

I grabbed the blue blanket from the rocking chair by the window and gently tossed it onto the bird, which had stunned itself when it hit the windowpane and landed on the floor. I scooped up the blanket and bird while speaking quietly and calmly, "Relax and be still, and I will gently set you free." I talked to the tiny, frightened bird in a lovingly tender way as though I were speaking to one of my children who had awakened from a bad dream. Hearing these words of hope and promise in my voice, I felt strangely warmed to the very core of my being in an indescribable way that I had never felt before.

"Be still! Be calm! Stop trying so hard! Let me help you!" The words reminded me of a prayer I had been reading earlier in the morning.

> *"God of Peace, who has promised that in returning and rest we shall be saved, in quietness and confidence shall be our strength. Lift me; I pray to the Presence of Thy Spirit, where I may be still and know that you are God."*

> — Episcopal Book of Common Prayer, page 832.

I carried the bird to the front door and released it to freedom from its terror. I put the pills back in the bottle with shaking hands and made myself a cup of tea. Bird or Angel?

CHAPTER SEVENTEEN

Hope and Healing

The bird was my sign of hope and I believed that just as I had helped the bird, God would help me. It was time to try a new doctor. A friend suggested a young doctor who took a holistic approach. He had his office in the next town. He was a Chiropractic Nutritionist, Dr. Tim Davis, a Christian who had helped someone she knew. I made an appointment.

I made another appointment with another new doctor who had just set up his practice in town. He was an internist. We hoped someone could help me understand what was happening and restore my health.

After blood and hair samples were taken, results showed I had food and chemical sensitivities, which caused my stomach problems. I was sensitive to natural gas and petroleum products. Our home had a gas stove in the kitchen. We also had a gas furnace in a closet close to our bedroom. We called to have our home inspected, and they found a crack in the furnace. Natural gas was leaking into our living space and would eventually harm us all. The natural gas leak caused headaches, dizziness, trouble breathing, depression, and anxiety. I tell myself these many years later that I was the family's unbeknownst canary and this situation alerted us to the danger of the gas leak for all of us.

I was prescribed a new diet and vitamin supplements to restore my health, I had lost a lot of weight and was down to 105 pounds which is underweight for a woman of 5'6."

The new internist in town assured me I was not crazy. He explained he had written his thesis on a condition that presented missed beats, fluttering heart rate, and dizziness. These were the same symptoms that my grandmother had lived with her whole life so it might be genetic. He set me up for an appointment for an electrocardiogram and an echocardiogram of my heart. The tests confirmed a prolapsed mitral valve. He wrote me a prescription for a beta-blocker to control the rapid heart rate and missed beats.

After several months, my health stabilized, and I could see that the bird in February was a definite turning point in my health and quality of life for myself and my family. Was it just a bird or an angel?

> *"Because you are my help, I sing in the shadow of your wings. My soul clings to you; your right hand upholds me."*

> — Psalm 63:7-8. 7 , NIV Study Bible 1985

Dad, Mom, Myself and baby Jade.

Julia Laura Falconeri Gorecki Hite

June 1898–November 1992

Strong Maternal Grandmother…
memories lovingly remain
for this little *babushka* woman
who seemed so out of sync
with my world.

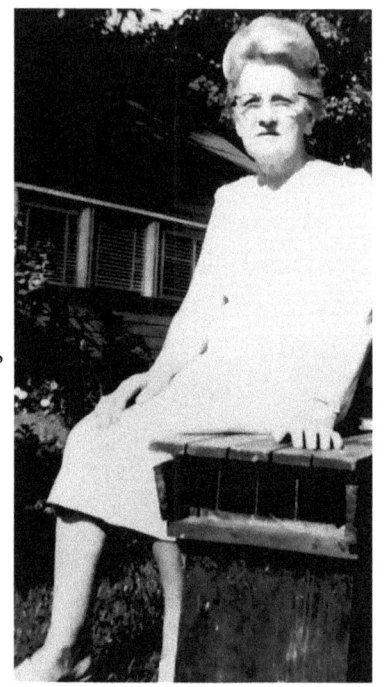

Inwardly, I'd smile, amused,
at her awkward, "OLD COUNTRY" ways,
unusual references,
occasional words and phrases spoken,
in a language, I had no desire to learn.
Who needed Polish in the 50's
When I was a child
or the '60s
When I was a teenage girl?

A blouse was a waist.
A closet a press.
A fridge was an ice box.

Cotton-candy hair,
pulled back tight,
done up in a twist or a knot.
Loose powder's sweet aroma and sparkling blue eyes,
softened the gnarly knuckles and *Harlow* brows
penciled dark and thin.

Devoutly committed to her faith,
her sterling silver beads rattled in her pocketed hand,
as she walked toward her centennial.

She had so little,
she gave me so much.
No words of wisdom
or way to heal
the family pain…

So, she worked hard, determined
to keep us clothed and fed
when our parents failed.

We were the fortunate recipients
Of her *Goodwill* finds
as proof of her love for us.
Her creativity with cotton or wool,
her passion for stitchery,
kept those bony, arthritic fingers busy
long after she could barely see.
She had me thread the needles
that deftly flew binding the fabric
and us together.

Kocham Cię — I love you
GTW 2016

About the Author

Gail and her husband, Steve have been married for 55 years. They live in South Carolina enjoying the mountains and the coast and being close to their two daughters, seven grandchildren and four great grandchildren.

Gail has worked in Early Childhood Education for 30 years as a Teacher or Director and presently teaches art to four and five-year-olds at her daughter's Christian Preschool. Her love for children is evident in her two children's books that emphasize the love of God in a delightful way that children can enjoy and understand. Her children's books are entitled *Gifts of Love* and *Child of Stardust*.